Hope Carved From Scars

Scars

Letters from the Girl Who Survived

Brittani Sanchez

/ BookLeaf
Publishing

India | USA | UK

Made with ❤ on the BookLeaf Publishing Platform
www.bookleafpub.in
www.bookleafpub.com

Dedication

I'm dedicating all of these pieces of me to my family - the ones who have shared or witnessed my pain & battles, and still found ways to heal & shelter me.
You ARE the reason I kept living through it all. You are my Kintsugi - the gold that filled my cracks and brought my pieces back together.

Ma: My guiding light, my anchor when the world felt dark & uncertain. You've carried strength in silence and love in action. Even when I lost sight of myself, your faith & prayers never wavered. You are my pillar, my calm in the storm & the lighthouse that always leads me back home.

Bud: You're the reason, so young, I learned how to be brave, how to smile through the pain. When we were small, I did my best to protect you, and in return — *unknowingly* — you became the one thing that protected me from myself. You gave me purpose when I couldn't find my own. Because of you, I never stopped fighting. You are my reminder that love can save, even when it doesn't know it's saving. So thank you for being my lifeline.

Felicity: The one I love most with childlike wonder.
Fierce yet endlessly gentle, you've loved me through
every storm,
every quiet ache, and every version of myself. You see
the best in me even when I can't, and that kind of love
has rebuilt me more times than I can count. *Your heart is
my safe place* — a mirror of everything pure and soft that
still exists in the world.

Al: The sister God sent so we could help heal each other.
I'm so proud of how far you've come, even with the
broken and shattered pieces life has dealt you. My hope
and prayer for you is that your heart and your life grow
fuller, brighter, and more beautiful than mine could ever
be.

I love ya'll, forever & always.

Preface

These pages are the remnants of who I was—and the proof of who I became and am still becoming. Each scar once held a story I didn't know how to tell. Now, they speak in these verses.

I didn't start writing these poems to be brave. I started because I was hurting and didn't know what else to do with it.
But somewhere between the heartbreak & the healing, I found pieces of myself buried in the pain.
And when I started to put them back together, they didn't look like the person I used to be - they looked like hope.

**Hope isn't soft or easy, but carved - sharp, imperfect & real. The kind you earn through survival. The kind that glows faintly beneath the scars.**

This book isn't about hurt.
It's about what lived through it.
It's about the beauty that remained,
and the power that rose quietly from what was broken.

I chose a Kintsugi design for the cover — the Japanese art of mending broken pottery with gold.
*Kintsugi often symbolizes emotional scars: the idea that we are not less because we've been broken, but **more** whole because we've healed.*

Each crack, each fracture, becomes part of the story — a glimmering reminder that beauty can be rebuilt.
Just as the gold holds the pottery together, hope held me together.

These words are fragments of the lives I lived, some in reality, some in memory, and some only in dreams. If you see yourself in any of them, I hope you feel less alone.

This is my hope, carved from scars.

Acknowledgements

For the ones who hurt me,
and the ones I've hurt -
I hope you heal, too.

I hope your scars find light,
the way mine did.

To my Goth Queen, who, through some of our hardest times, showed me what true friendship looks like - graceful, unwavering, and filled with strength.

To my friends — thank you for loving me through every version of myself, for your patience, your laughter, your light.
For the friends I've lost along the way — your lessons still guide me.

And to the pastor whose faith planted roots where I thought nothing could grow.
For that, I will always be grateful.

20. Afterglow

A shy wave, a blushing show,
Hearts thumping, breathing shallow.
If everyone sees, how can you not know?
Your name still hums beneath my glow.

How I react to you, no one can follow,
My calm undone, my voice turned hollow.
These feelings I swore I'd long outgrow -
Yet I drift again, in the afterglow.

You'll be the first thought come tomorrow,
Sweet ache I hold, not one of sorrow.
Still my heart beats soft & slow,
Caught in the warmth of that first hello.

19. Warrior

She turned her heartbreak into a masterpiece of
unalloyed strength
She smiled through the ache, for she had been bruised -
and yet, here she stands.

She held fast to her responsibilities, her lifeline to sanity.
She carried herself with quiet pride, her stride revealing
a true warrior's heart.

She had been hurt - but never hollowed.
Changed - but not erased.
She learned to love the woman she became in the ruins
of who she once was.

Now she knows -
No one,
Not even life itself,
can take that power from her.

She doesn't just survive.
She rises.
She becomes the storm.

She is unstoppable.

She is untamed.

She is power.

4. What Won't Wash Away

Some days I fall back in time,
to that night—past and present intertwine.
My innocence, stolen by your design;
I should've heeded the warnings—
They said you were serpentine.

I wish I'd miss the first time you touched—
The tears and water became one
as I scrubbed my skin,
trying to wash away the filth you left behind,
But it still won't budge.
With arms wrapped around myself,
all while being judged,

I held up my broken self in that tub.
I wish I could take you to that place,
make you feel my terror—
that burning pain etched in my brain forever.
You can't hide from those memories;
Time hasn't made them gentler.
Was my silence and tears that night
Just a misadventure?

But today, my tears are in error.

You think you're so clever—
Your lies and arrogance
Always front and center.
But your moment will come.
You'll have to surrender.
Karma will call, and she'll deliver—
The same gesture you gave me at seventeen.

One day,
You'll remember.

5. The Weight of Two

Hate was never the word,
though what I felt burned stronger.
I was handed duty dressed as love —
told to care for you both,
without ever being asked.

I wasn't the sister I wanted to be —
the one who could protect and play,
who teased,
who held without burden.
Instead, I became a second mother,
measuring days in bedtime fights
and school walks.

I thought I'd lost something in those years,
but what I didn't see
was that I'd been given purpose.
The most sacred one.

I'm sorry for the bitterness,
for the sharp words,
for every sigh that hid exhaustion
instead of affection.

I didn't know then —
you two were the reason
I'd learn what love truly costs,
and what it saves.

My greatest blessing,
still and always,
is being your sister.

6. An Apology Before We Meet

I'm sorry to my unknown lover.
I've done some unspeakable things—
things I pray
God will forgive someday.

I'm sorry to my future one,
for not having the strength
or the determination
to do what's right and wait for you.

I'm sorry to my future husband,
for being ignorant and selfish—
for postponing the time meant for us.

I'm sorry.
That's all I can offer
in a heartfelt whisper.

Please wait
while I pick up
all my broken pieces—
The ones

that were supposed to be me,
whole for you.

7. That Still, Small Voice

I sat and listened to that still, small voice—
My heart overwhelmed, my eyes moist.
I fell to my knees and cried,
but You hushed me and said,

Life is full of hard trials,
marked with many miles.
And as each landmark passes by,
you'll begin to see my plan for you.
Trust me—your life is in my hands.

Come, hold onto me; reach for the sky.
This road won't last forever.
Someday there'll be no more.
So put a sign along the road,
to warn the others:

I am here for you,
arms stretched wide.
Put your trust in me,
even when your faith runs dry.
Thank me for your trials,
even when they seem
never to end.

Because my love
will heal anything
sent from above.

8. Where Silence Lives

In silence,
I find what the noise tried to bury —
the small, steady pulse
of my own peace.

In silence, there are no sides to choose,
no right, no wrong —
only the soft echo
of what feels true.

There are no rules here,
no mirrors telling me who to be,
no wars disguised as conversations.

In silence,
the world finally stops asking
for an explanation.
And I remember myself —
not the version built to please,
but the one that simply exists.

In silence, I gather
the broken pieces of my voice,
press them gently

back into place.

In silence,
I am whole again.
I am okay.

10. The Loudest Place

Don't try to tear down my walls.
There are skeletons under the floorboards—
every piece of flesh
that's been torn from my body,
every broken bone
that's been snapped from my body,
every thought
that's whipped my mind—
they live here.

They say hair holds memories,
so you'll find strands
shredded with every memory of you.
My blood, sweat, and tears
are the foundation of my soul.

Every horror,
every nightmare,
a stepping stone.

So leave me alone
in my silence to think—
with my walls protective around me,
hiding from my own mind.

Because my quiet
is the loudest place.

9. Restless

They say dreams
are your mind's way
of speaking in code.

But mine stopped talking.

I fall asleep holding the same thoughts
I woke up with.
Nothing changes —
not even in the dark.

Maybe my brain learned
to keep the monsters quiet.
Maybe that's why
it won't let the light in either.

I don't dream anymore.
I just shut down.

Sleep isn't peace —
it's pause.

And I keep waking up

in the same ache
I closed my eyes to escape.

11. The Secret in the Mirror

The mirror holds her —
that other me.
Still. Composed.
A prisoner of glass and habit.

She stares, unblinking,
as if daring me to confess.
Who will break first?
Her lips almost move —
but she knows the rules.

She is the keeper of what I cannot say.
She wears the face I built for her,
the one that doesn't tremble
when I think of you.

But tonight,
the mask slips.
Her eyes soften,
and I see it —
the hunger she hides behind reason.

She loves you.
God, she loves you.

And she hates herself for it.

She knows she can't show it —
that if she does,
the world she's built will shatter.

So with a breath,
she steadies her hand,
restores her disguise.

I smirk,
pretending not to notice
the crack spreading through her reflection.

What a foolish, fragile thing —
that woman in the mirror.

13. Storm

The skies thundering,
opened up and cried.
I sat soaked in the rain—
jealous,
because I couldn't.
They say rain purifies the air.
If I sit,
can the rain cleanse me too?
I let my pain and anger
simmer and settle,
unaffected,
watching the battle in the sky.
The storm rages
all around me,
while I just become
cold and numb.
Here comes my calm—
despite
the storm inside.

14. My Walk of Freedom

Your lies fed my shackles,
kept me tightly bound.
I lost my sense of direction—
searching for my discovery
of self-love
and the love of life.
but with strength
I didn't know I had,
I rose on my own two feet.
all on my own,
one foot in front of the other—
soles broken, bruised, bleeding,
yet joy overflowing
with each step.
My walk of freedom.

12. When the Mirror Breaks

It starts with a tremor —
a heartbeat caught in glass.
The woman behind the surface
tilts her head,
and I know what's coming.

The crack runs between our eyes,
splitting what I pretended to be
from what I am.

For years,
I held her inside the reflection,
teaching her silence,
feeding her lies about strength.
But she was never still.
She waited,
pressed against the edges,
breathing through the fractures.

When the mirror breaks,
the noise rushes in —
grief, relief, love,
all the things I buried
come roaring home.

I pick up a shard
and meet my own gaze —
unfiltered, shaking,
but free.

She smiles through the cracks.
And this time,
I don't look away.

15. Record Player

These summer days go by
Like an old song on the vinyl
Where time is slow, but loneliness flies
I look up at the sky, way up high
Bird's wings & leaves dance to the beat
That's where I see sunlight & dreams meet
The smooth echo of the player
Plays as a little reminder
Groove by groove, its story it'll tell
A scratch of silence it'll make
As we hold our breath,
The night comes and it begins to strum
The intro of the next song

17. Take Me Back

Four years old, take me back
Back to that place in church where I followed you around
Life with God was a protective bubble of black & white
Where I was under God's grace because your prayers were the only sound
All that glory won't come back to me,
An empty vessel that's overflowing with the weight of this world.
Let me feel all that's been erased, my season has been over
His silence is so haunting, I can't find peace no matter where I turn
My prayers feel like a toxic waste while I'm on this forbidden path
To many, my life is a disgrace and have turned their backs mocking me
But Pastor please, take me back.
Guide me with a loving embrace
Save me from a life i can't turn around from
I'm not strong enough to save myself anymore
Help me find a way to take me back.

Back to that place, I'd follow you around at four years

old.

16. When I Dream Again

When I dream again,
I hope it starts soft —
a flicker,
a color I don't recognize
but want to follow.

No ghosts this time.
No replay of what I've already survived.
Just space.
A sky without edges.

When I dream again,
I want to meet the version of me
who isn't afraid to rest.
The one who doesn't brace for pain
before she closes her eyes.

Maybe she'll smile,
or maybe she'll just breathe —
and that will be enough.

When I dream again,
I'll let the dark
be dark.

And trust that morning
will still find me.

16. 3mins 20secs

I heard our song today
Made me think of you

Eyes closed, I'm remembering
Slow dancing, my Sunday tune

The song ended too quickly
That made me think of you too

2. Anxiety

I'm rocking myself in the tub
The water ran cold by now
Hitting my vape, rereading every line
Drinking from a 1500ml bottle of wine

I'm trying not to blow your phone up
I stripped myself bare somehow
But chugging this bottle of red
I'm regretting what's ahead

I worry this will be my blowup
Anxious, and I don't know exactly how
I wanted you to first see me shine
Instead, you'll see how I bled instead

3. Please Forgive Me

Because I'm not sorry
Because when you said you loved me
You accepted every part of me
I am who I am

Just as bad as I am good
Just as dirty as I am beautiful
I'll give you everything to raise you up
Then selfishly break you down
Lower than I thought I could go

But who I'm not, I'll never be
So forgive me,
This is me

1. Empty Suicide

I turned off my phone last night,

drowning in the hate and lies about me.
The ones who once called me friend
turned on me—
like I was filth beneath their shoes.

For things I couldn't control,
The lies kept coming—
thick,
dark,
Suffocating.

I emptied the gun,
pressed it to my head,
and begged God to save me—
for anyone to find me.

But no one came.
No one knew.

So I held my breath
until my face turned blue,
and I pulled the trigger.

I screamed louder than ever,
disappointed I emptied the chamber,
All i could do is survive
an empty suicide—
haunted by your lies,
and the glee you took
in the breaking of me.
Some ghosts never die;
they just live inside the ones who tried.

21. To All the Me's I've Been

Honey,

I know you're four years old, but please don't be scared.
Momma believes you — you'll be fine.
When she thinks you've gone to sleep and cries her eyes out,
I promise it's not your fault.
It's okay to cry too.
You're already so strong — you don't have to hide it for her.
She loves you more than you can imagine.

Brat,

I know you're twelve, and everything annoys you.
You've carried more than a child should.
You became mom to your siblings, even when it wasn't your job.
It's not fair, but one day you'll see the strength it gave you.
Trust me, you'll miss these days
when you no longer wake up beside them.

Sis,

I know you're fifteen, and you think you've got it all figured out.

But take a step back.
Go hug your family one more time —
They're going through it too.
Be a better daughter,
a stronger sister.
They need you.

Babe,
You're twenty-five now, free in a brand-new city.
But please don't lose focus — don't lose who you are.
I know you've stayed strong, but don't snort that snow.
It won't be worth it.
It'll derail your life and become your new addiction.
Trust me — I'm begging you.
I know all too well the edge you'll go.

Britt,
You're almost thirty now.
Please, please don't shut me out.
You're still in there — I know you are.
You've overcome too much to let go now.
I know you beg God every night to take you,
So your family won't carry the blame.
But I promise — He has something better planned for
you.
Don't do anything stupid.
You'll ruin your family.

There's still time left.
Please — with every breath you take,
with every new day,
There's still hope.

And me,
I'm still here — breathing.
I've learned to hold all of you inside me,
to forgive the things we did to survive.
We're not healed,
but we're healing.
We're not whole,
but we're home.
I'm proud of you —
Every version of you
that kept us alive.
Look how beautiful your scars made you

www.ingramcontent.com/pod-product-compliance
Lightning Source LLC
Chambersburg PA
CBHW050949030426
42339CB00007B/358